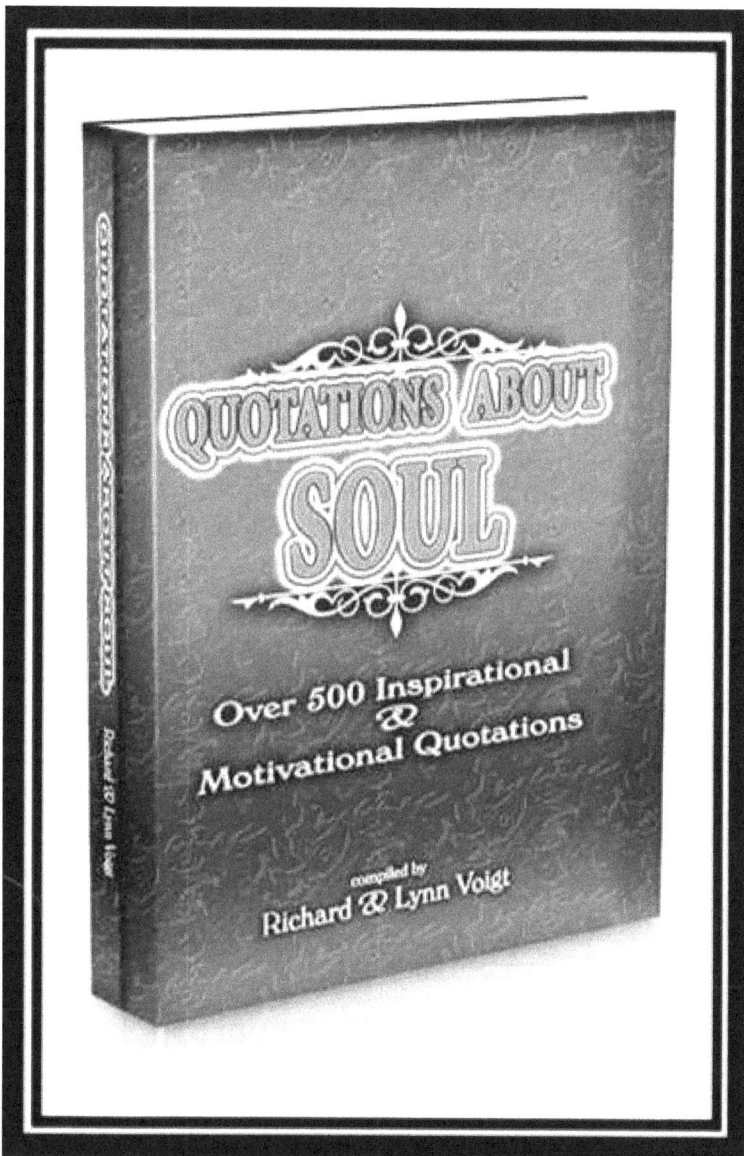

QUOTATIONS ABOUT
SOUL

Over 500 Inspirational
&
Motivational Quotations

compiled by
Richard & Lynn Voigt

Quotations About Soul
500 Inspirational & Motivational Quotations About Soul

ISBN-13: 978-1-940961-16-3
ISBN-10: 1940961165

Cover Art by RIVOart Studios

First Printing, 2014

Printed in the United States of America

To Access More Powerful Marketing Tools Visit:

www.RIVObooks.com

www.RIVOinc.com

www.10000DailyLeads.com

Quotations About
SOUL

500 Inspirational & Motivational Quotations About Soul

-.|.-•.*'''''*.•._-.|.-•**•-.|.-•.*'''''*.•-.|.-

Compiled by
Richard & Lynn Voigt
Education Specialists

Introduction:

Most people use the word Soul when referring to something they have difficulty describing. Yet most people believe the Soul is a non-physical entity, unlike the heart and other body parts.

Here's our inspirational and motivational collection of over 500 quotations about Soul starting back in Plato's time, to contemporary authors, artists, poets, musicians, philosophers, world leaders of today, and those unique thinkers currently posting quotations on social media.

If you ever wondered how to clarify your Soul and where it resides, these quotations will quickly open your eyes in understanding what great minds have written about the concept of Soul.

Many struggle to define or clarify exactly what role the Soul plays in their own life. Others believe it is an important and powerful part of their spiritual being meant to compliment and balance the physical and intellectual entities of the human body.

One of the aspects of quotations that we enjoy is seeing how others throughout history have taken time to describe the energy of Soul.

You can open this book to any page as you start or end each day and find a quotation that brings a smile to your heart. You may even want to create and share a series of Postnotes™ and anonymously post them around your apartment, home or at the office and see whose day you'll brighten.

This book will soon become your favorite companion, especially for those who appreciate positive thoughts that can easily brighten a morning, afternoon, or evening. You'll probably find yourself wanting to share a new found quotation with family and friends or simply find the perfect quotation for those who may be going through a very difficult time or just need a little inspirational or motivational pick-me-up.

As you read these amazing thoughts, it is our hope that you will be inspired to start writing your own quotations about what the concept of Soul means to you and how it guides your core values.

And when you do create your own Soul quotation, we would love to have you send it to us, so that we can add it to future updates of this book publication. We will definitely credit your name as the author as we have done throughout this book where the author is know.

Send your quotation to support@RIVObooks.com

In the meantime, we think you'll thoroughly enjoy this unique collection of over 500 Quotations about Soul. Without further delay, we invite you to enjoy reading our Soul collection of quotations.

"May Your Life's Journey Lead You To The Path
You Seek That Illuminates And Enlightens Your
Soul In Finding The Meaning To Your Life"
- Richard Marvin Voigt

"One Of The Hardest Tasks Is To Extract Continually From One's Soul An Almost Inexhaustible Ill Will" - Victor Hugo

"The Soul Which Has No Fixed Purpose In Life Is Lost; To Be Everywhere, Is To Be Nowhere" - Michel De Montaigne

"Discipline Is The Soul Of An Army. It Make Small Numbers Formidable; Procures Success To The Weak, And Esteem To All" - George Washington

"A Moment Comes, Which Comes But Rarely In History, When We Step Out From The Old To The New; When An Age Ends; And When The Soul Of A Nation Long Suppressed Finds Utterance" - Jawaharlal Nehru

"If It Be A Sin To Covet Honor, I Am The Most Offending Soul" - William Shakespeare

"To Know What You Prefer Instead Of Humbly Saying Amen To What The World Tells You Ought To Prefer, Is To Have Kept Your Soul Alive" - Robert Louis Stevenson

"Who Ever Is Out Of Patience Is Out Of Possession Of Their Soul" - Francis Bacon

"Do You Not See How Necessary A World Of
Pains And Troubles Is To School An
Intelligence And Make It A Soul"
- John Keats

"Art Is The Stored Honey Of The Human Soul,
Gathered On Wings Of Misery And Travail"
- Theodore Dreiser

"One Certainly Has A Soul; But How It Came
To Allow Itself To Be Enclosed In A Body
Is More Than I Can Imagine. I Only Know
If Once Mine Gets Out, I'll Have A Bit Of
A Tussle Before I Let It Get In Again
To That Of Any Other"
- Lord Byron

"The Man Of Virtuous Soul Commands Not,
Nor Obeys" - Percy Bysshe Shelley

"Lightness, Jesting, And Joking, Can Only Be
Indulged At The Expense Of Barrenness Of
Soul, And The Loss Of The Favor Of God"
- Ellen G. White

"I Think You Have To Know Who You Are. Get
To Know The Monster That Lives In Your Soul,
Dive Deep Into Your Soul And Explore It"
- Tori Amos

"Twas But My Tongue, 'Twas Not My Soul
That Swore" - Euripides

"Literature, Not Scripture, Sustains The Mind
And - Since There Is No Other Metaphor - Also
The Soul" - Christopher Hitchens

"Depression Begins With Disappointment.
When Disappointment Festers In Our Soul,
It Leads To Discouragement" - Joyce Meyer

"What Is Art? It Is The Response Of Man's
Creative Soul To The Call Of The Real"
- Rabindranath Tagore

"Friendship Is The Marriage Of The Soul, And
This Marriage Is Liable To Divorce" - Voltaire
"To Finish A Work? To Finish A Picture? What
Nonsense! To Finish It Means To Be Through
With It, To Kill It, To Rid It Of Its Soul, To Give It
Its Final Blow The Coup De Grace For The
Painter As Well As For The Picture"
- Pablo Picasso

-

"There Is No Faculty Of The Human Soul So
Persistent And Universal As That Of Hatred."
- Henry Ward Beecher

"Alone Let Him Constantly Meditate In Solitude On That Which Is Salutary For His Soul, For He Who Meditates In Solitude Attains Supreme Bliss" - Guru Nanak

"There Is One Knows Not What Sweet Mystery About This Sea, Whose Gently Awful Stirrings Seem To Speak Of Some Hidden Soul Beneath" - Herman Melville

"There Is No Person That Love Cannot Heal; There Is No Soul That Love Cannot Save" - Carlos Santana

"This Soul, Or Life Within Us, By No Means Agrees With The Life Outside Us. If One Has The Courage To Ask Her What She Thinks, She Is Always Saying The Very Opposite To What Other People Say" - Miguel Angel Ruiz

-

"A Room Without Books Is Like A Body Without A Soul" - Marcus Tullius Cicero

"Tears Are The Summer Showers To The Soul" - Alfred Austin

"Upturned Toward The Sun, Eyes Closed. That Color And Warmth I See And Feel Is The Soul On Fire. If Only It Remained When Again My Eyes Opened" - Jeb Dickerson

"All Things Must Come To The Soul From Its Roots, From Where It Is Planted"
-    Saint Teresa Of Avila

"When You're In Touch With Our Soul, Our Hearts Won't Ever Lead Us Wrong. Keep That Road Open And It'll Take You To Wonderful Places You Can Only Imagine"
-    Tracy Campanella

"What Sculpture Is To A Block Of Marble, Education Is To The Soul" - Joseph Addison

"One Thing In The World, Of Value, Is The Active Soul" - Ralph Waldo Emerson

"A Sad Soul Can Kill Quicker Than A Germ"
-    John Steinbeck

"The Soul Is Placed In The Body Like A Rough Diamond, And Must Be Polished, Or The Luster Of It Will Never Appear" - Daniel Defoe

"There Is One Spectacle Grander That The Sea, That Is The Sky; There Is One Spectacle Grander Than The Sky, That Is The Interior Of The Soul" - Victor Hugo

"The Heart Of A Human Being Is No Different From The Soul Of Heaven And Earth. In Your Practice Always Keep In Your Thoughts The Interaction Of Heaven And Earth, Water And Fire, Yin And Yang" - Morihei Ueshiba

"The Thoughtful Soul To Solitude Retires" - Omar Khayyam

"One Loss Is Good For The Soul, Too Many Losses Is Not Good For The Coach" - Knute Rockne
-
"Beautiful Music Is The Art Of Prophets That Can Calm The Agitations Of The Soul; It Is One Of The Most Magnificent And Delightful Presents God Has Given Us" - Martin Luther

"Whoever Knows It Also Knows That In Love There Is No More And No Less; But That He Who Loves Can Only Love With The Whole Heart, And With The Whole Soul; With All His Strength And With All His Will" - Max Muller

"At The End Of The Day You Will Not Remember The Person With The Most Beautiful Face But You Will Remember The Person With The Most Beautiful Heart And Soul" - Unknown

"Design Is The Fundamental Soul Of A
Man-Made Creation That Ends Up Expressing
Itself In Successive Outer Layers Of The
Product Or Service. The iMac Is Not Just The
Color Or Translucence Or The Shape Of The
Shell. The Essence Of The iMac Is To Be The
Finest Possible Consumer Computer In Which
Each Element Plays Together" - Steve Jobs

"Singing Is A Way Of Releasing An Emotion
That You Sometimes Can't Portray When
You're Acting. And Music Moves Your Soul,
So Music Is The Source Of The Most Intense
Emotions You Can Feel. When You Hear
A Song And You're Acting It's Incredible.
But When You're Singing A Song And
You're Acting It's Even More Incredible"
- Amanda Seyfried

"Valor Is Stability, Not Of Legs And Arms, But
Of Courage And The Soul"
- Michel De Montaigne

"I Suppose, In A Way, This Has Become Part
Of My Soul. It Is A Symbol Of My Life.
Whatever I Have Done That Really Matters,
I've Done Wearing It. When The Time Comes,
It Will Be In This That I Journey Forth.
What Greater Honor Could Come
To An American, And A Soldier"
- Douglas Macarthur

"Developing The Muscles Of The Soul Demands No Competitive Spirit, No Killer Instinct, Although It May Erect Pain Barriers That The Spiritual Athlete Must Crash Through" - Germaine Greer

"Old Age Is Far More Than White Hair, Wrinkles, The Feeling That It Is Too Late And The Game Finished, That The Stage Belongs To The Rising Generations. The True Evil Is Not The Weakening Of The Body, But The Indifference Of The Soul"
- Andre Maurois

"When The Whole World Has Their Eyes On You, If You Say Something That Doesn't Truly Come From Your Spirit And Your Soul, Or If You Wear Something That Doesn't Come From Your Spirit And Your Soul, It's An Injustice To Your Position. And So, I'm Really Myself Every Single Day And I Do It Because I Know My Fans Would Want Me To" - Lady Gaga

"To Go To The World Below, Having A Soul Which Is Like A Vessel Full Of Injustice, Is The Last And Worst Of All The Evils" - Plato

"Genius - To Know Without Having Learned; To Draw Just Conclusions From Unknown Premises; To Discern The Soul Of Things"
- Ambrose Bierce

"Music Is The Movement Of Sound To Reach
The Soul For The Education Of Its Virtue"
-    Plato

"For The People Who Ostensibly Wish Me Well
Or Are Worried About My Immortal Soul,
I Say I Take It Kindly"
- Christopher Hitchens

"Trust Your Soul" - A.D. Williams

"What Is Soul? It's Like Electricity - We Don't
Really Know What It Is, But It's A Force That
Can Light A Room" - Ray Charles

"Faith And Prayer Are The Vitamins Of The
Soul; Man Cannot Live In Health Without
Them" - Mahalia Jackson

"When You Do Things From Your Soul You
Feel A River Moving In You, A Joy.
When Action Come From Another Section,
The Feeling Disappears" - Rumi

"The Body Of A Sensualist Is The Coffin Of
A Dead Soul" - Christian Nestell Bovee

"The Momentous Thing In Human Life Is The
Art Of Winning The Soul To Good Or Evil"
- Francis Bacon

"Pregnancy Is A Kind Of Miracle. Especially So In That It Proves That A Man And Woman Can Conspire To Force God To Create A New Soul" - Robert Anton Wilson

"Most Laws Condemn The Soul And Pronounce Sentence. The Result Of The Law Of My God Is Perfect. It Condemns But Forgives. It Restores - More Than Abundantly - What It Takes Away" - Jim Elliot

"Bondage Is Of The Mind; Freedom Too Is Of The Mind. If You Say 'I Am A Free Soul. I Am A Son Of God Who Can Bind Me' Free You Shall Be" - Ramakrishna

"Electric Communication Will Never Be A Substitute For The Face Of Someone Who With Their Soul Encourages Another Person To Be Brave And True" - Charles Dickens

"The Good Critic Is He Who Relates The Adventures Of His Soul Among Masterpieces" - Anatole France

"If You're Losing Your Soul And You Know It, Then You've Still Got A Soul Left To Lose" - Charles Bukowski

"Frisbeetarianism Is The Belief That When You
Die, Your Soul Goes Up On The Roof
And Gets Stuck" - George Carlin

"I Can Say, 'Well, I'm A Male. I'm A Male
Human. I'm A Medical Doctor. I'm An Author...
If I Go To A Religious Point Of View, I Will Say,
'I Am A Soul. I Am A Spirit.' If I Go Into Science,
I Will Say, 'I Am Energy. I Am Light.' But
The Truth Is I Have No Idea What I Am"
- Miguel Angel Ruiz

"Dreams Are Illustrations From The Book
Your Soul Is Writing About You"
- Marsha Norman

"My Soul Is Nothing Now But The Dream
Dreamt By Matter Struggling With Itself"
- Paul Valery

"Learning How To Operate A Soul Figures To
Take Time" - Timothy Leary

"Only Man Knows What It Is Like To Be
Defeated And Reach Down To The Bottom
Of His Soul And Come Up With The Extra
Ounce Of Power It Takes To Win
When The Match Is Even"
- Muhammad Ali

"Nothing Can Be Compared To The Great Beauty And Capabilities Of A Soul; However Keen Our Intellects May Be, They Are As Unable To Comprehend Them As To Comprehend God, For, As He Has Told Us, He Created Us In His Own Image And Likeness"
-   Saint Teresa Of Avila

"One May Have A Blazing Hearth In One's Soul And Yet No One Ever Came To Sit By It. Passers-By See Only A Wisp Of Smoke From The Chimney And Continue On Their Way"
-   Vincent Van Gogh

"Just As The Soul Fills The Body, So God Fills The World. Just As The Soul Bears The Body, So God Endures The World. Just As The Soul Sees But Is Not Seen, So God Sees But Is Not Seen. Just As The Soul Feeds The Body, So God Gives Food To The World"
-   Marcus Tullius Cicero
-
"The Whole Course Of Human History May Depend On A Change Of Heart In One Solitary And Even Humble Individual - For It Is In The Solitary Mind And Soul Of The Individual That The Battle Between Good And Evil Is Waged And Ultimately Won Or Lost" - M. Scott Peck

"The Dancer's Body Is Simply The Luminous Manifestation Of The Soul" - Isadora Duncan

"Once Conform, Once Do What Other People Do Because They Do It, And Lethargy Steals Over All The Finer Nerves And Faculties Of The Soul. She Becomes All Outer Show And Inward Emptiness; Dull, Callous, And Indifferent" - Virginia Woolf

"It Is Only The Individual That A Soul Is Given" - Albert Einstein

"Nation' Was One That I'd Have Killed Myself If I Hadn't Written It. It Was Absolutely Important To Me That I Wrote It. It Was Good For My Soul" - Terri Pratchett

"Heaven Will Be Inherited By Every Man Who Has Heaven In His Soul" - Henry Ward Beecher

"Age Wrinkles The Body, Quitting Wrinkles The Soul" - Douglas MacArthur

"The Weakness Of A Soul Is Proportionate To The Number Of Truths That Must Be Kept From It" - Eric Hoffer

"Impressionism Is The Newspaper Of The Soul" - Henri Matisse

"The Only Justice Is To Follow The Sincere
Intuition Of The Soul, Angry Or Gentle. Anger Is
Just, And Pity Is Just, But Judgement Is Never
Just" - D. H. Lawrence

"Humanity Gives, A Soul To The Universe,
Wings To The Mind, Flight To The Imagination
And Life To Everything"
- Sunny Gupta

"When I Admire The Wonders Of A Sunset
Or The Beauty Of The Moon,
My Soul Expands In The Worship
Of The Creator"
- Mahatma Gandhi

"Confession Is Good For The Conscience,
But It Usually Bypasses The Soul"
- Mignon Mclaughlin

"When I Took The Habit, The Lord Immediately
Showed Me How He Favours Those
Who Do Violence To Themselves In Order To
Serve Him. No One Saw What I Endured... At
The Moment Of My Entrance Into This New
State I Felt A Joy So Great That It Has Never
Failed Me Even To This Day; And God
Converted The Dryness Of My Soul
Into A Very Great Tenderness"
- Saint Teresa Of Avila

"After Every Strom The Sun Will Smile;
For Every Problem There Is A Solution,
And The Soul's Indefeasible Duty Is
To Be Of Good Cheer"
- William R. Alger

"I See Dance Being Used As Communication
Between Body And Soul, To Express
What It Too Deep To Find For Words"
- Ruth St. Denis

"Imagination Is The Eye Of The Soul"
- Joseph Joubert

"Every Gardener Touches The Soul Of Mother
Earth With Each Seed They Sow Or Plant"
- Richard Marvin Voigt

"The Soul Never Thinks Without A Picture"
- Aristotle

"Re-Examine All That You Have
BeenTold....Dismiss That
Which Insults Your Soul"
- Walt Whitman

"Soul Shadows You Everywhere"
- Terri Guillemets

"I Met In The Street A Very Poor Young Man Who Was In Love. His Hat Was Old, His Coat Worn, His Cloak Was Out At The Elbows, The Water Passed Through His Shoes, And The Stars Through His Soul" - Victor Hugo

"There Is No Chance, No Destiny, No Fate, That Can Circumvent Or Hinder Or Control The Firm Resolve Of A Determined Soul"
- Ella Wheeler Wilcox

"The Moment I First Heard Love I Gave Up My Soul, My Heart, And My Eyes"
- Rumi

"When You Touch Someone's Life It Is A Privilege. When You Touch Someone's Heart It Is A Blessing. When You Touch Someone's Mind It Is An Honor. When You Touch Someone's Soul It Is A Triumph. When You Touch Someone's Spirit It Is A Miracle"
- Ritu Ghatourey

"Sarcasm: The Last Refuge Of Modest And Chaste-Souled People When The Privacy Of Their Soul Is Coarsely And Intrusively Invaded"
- Fyodor Dostoyevsky

"Flowers Are The Sweetest Things God Ever Made And Forgot To Put A Soul Into"
- Henry Ward Beecher

"The Value Of Life Can Be Measured
By How Many Times Your Soul
Has Been Deeply Stirred"
- Soichiro Honda

"There's A Part Of You - The Born-Again Part,
Your Spirit - That's Dead To Sin.
That's Why It Bothers You Now When You Sin.
The 'Wilderness' Part Of You - Your Soul
- Is Your Unrenewed Mind, Out-Of-Control
Emotions, And Stubborn Will"
- Joyce Meyer

"You Are A Beautiful Soul Hidden By
The Trench Coat Of The Ego"
- Mike Dolan

"Jealousy Is The Jaundice Of The Soul"
- Meister Eckhart

"How Strange A Thing This Is! The Priest
Telleth Me That The Soul Is Worth All The Gold
In The World, And The Merchants Say That It Is
Not Worth A Clipped Piece Of Silver"
- Oscar Wilde

"A Nation's Culture Resides In The Hearts
And In The Soul Of Its People"
- Mahatma Gandhi

"God Who Is Eternally Complete, Who Directs The Stars, Who Is The Master Of Fates, Who Elevates Man From His Lowliness To Himself, Who Speaks For The Cosmos To Every Single Human Soul, Is The Most Brilliant Manifestation Of The Goal Of Perfection" - Alfred Adler

"Blessed Is The Influence Of One True, Loving Human Soul On Another" - George Eliot
"Toughness Is In The Soul And Spirit, Not In Muscles" - Alex Karras

"This Is The Ultimate End Of Man, To Find The One Which Is In Him; Which Is His Truth, Which Is His Soul; The Key With Which He Opens The Gate Of The Spiritual Life, The Heavenly Kingdom" - Rabindranath Tagore

"Equality Is The Soul Of Liberty; There Is, In Fact, No Liberty Without It" - Frances Wright
"Let My Soul Smile Through My Heart And My Heart Smile Through My Eyes, That I May Scatter Rich Smiles In Sad Hearts"
- Paramahansa Yogananda

"I Was So Astonished That Another Had Penetrated So Deeply Into The Secrets Of My Soul, And That He Knew What I Did Not Know Myself, That When I Recovered From It He Had Already Been Long Upon The Street"
- Max Muller

"I Have Also Seen Children Successfully Surmounting The Effects Of An Evil Inheritance. That Is Due To Purity Being And Inherent Attribute Of The Soul"
- Mahatma Gandhi

"What Is Right For One Soul May Not Be Right For Another. It May Mean Having To Stand On Your Own And Do Something Strange In The Eyes Of Others" - Eileen Caddy

"The End Of Life Is To Be Like God, And The Soul Following God Will Be Like Him"
- Socrates

"Sin Is Whatever Obscures The Soul"
- Andre Gide

"Nothing Can So Pierce The Soul As The Uttermost Sigh Of The Body"
- George Santayana

"Every Conquering Temptation Represents A New Fund Of Moral Energy. Every Trial Endured And Weathered In The Right Spirit Makes A Soul Nobler And Stronger Than It Was Before" - William Butler Yeats

"There Are Words In The Soul Of A Newborn Baby, Wanting And Waiting To Be Written"
- Toba Beta

"I Don't Think Anyone, Until Their Soul Leaves
Their Body, Is Past The Point Of No Return"
- Tom Hiddleston

"Every Single Human Soul Has More Meaning
And Value Than The Whole Of History"
- Nikolai Berdyaev

"Good For The Body Is The Work Of The Body,
Good For The Soul The Work Of The Soul, And
Good For Either The Work Of The Other"
- Henry David Thoreau

"The Soul, Fortunately, Has An Interpreter
Often An Unconscious, But Still
A Truthful Interpreter - In The Eye"
- Charlotte Bronte

"If A Man Could Pass Through Paradise In A
Dream, And Have A Flower Presented To Him
As A Pledge That His Soul Had Really Been
There, And If He Found That Flower In His
Hand When He Awake - Aye, What Then"
- Samuel Taylor Coleridge

"Deliberation And Debate Is The Way You
Stir The Soul Of Our Democracy"
- Jesse Jackson

"One Looks Back With Appreciation To The
Brilliant Teachers, But With Gratitude To Those
Who Touched Our Human Feelings.
The Curriculum Is So Much Necessary Raw
Material, But Warmth Is The Vital Element For
The Growing Plant And For The Soul
Of The Child" - Carl Jung

"Let There Be Many Windows To Your Soul,
That All The Glory Of The World May
Beautify It" - Ella Wheeler Wilcox

"False Words Are Not Only Evil In Themselves,
But They Infect The Soul With Evil" - Socrates

"The Glory Of Gardening: Hands In The Dirt,
Head In The Sun, Heart With Nature.
To Nuture A Garden Is To Feed Not Just On
The Body, But The Soul" - Alfred Austin

"The Windows Of My Soul I Throw Wide Open
To The Sun" - John Greenlead Whittler

"If I Were Dammed Of Body And Soul, I Know
Whose Prayers Would Make Me Whole, Mother
O' Mine O Mother O' Mine" - Rudyard Kipling

"The Devil Has Put A Penalty On All Things We
Enjoy In Life. Either We Suffer In Health Or We
Suffer In Soul Or We Get Fat" - Albert Einstein

"Say Not, "I Have Found The Truth," But
Rather, "I Have Found A Truth." Say Not,
"I Have Found The Path Of The Soul."
Say Rather, "I Have Met The Soul Walking
Upon My Path." For The Soul Walks Upon
All Paths. The Soul Walks Not Upon A Line,
Neither Does It Grow Like A Reed.
The Soul Unfolds Itself, Like A Lotus
Of Countless Petals"
-   Khalil Gibran

"I Love Thee To The Depth And Breadth
And Height My Soul Can Reach"
- Elizabeth Barrett Browning

"It's Our Hearts And Brains That We Should
Exercise More Often. You Can Put On All The
Makeup You Want, But It Won't Make Your
Soul Pretty" - Kevyn Aucoin

"To Practice Five Things Under All
Circumstances Constitutes Perfect Virtue;
These Five Are Gravity, Generosity Of Soul,
Sincerity, Earnestness, And Kindness"
- Confucious

"I Have No Companion But Love, No
Beginning, No End, No Dawn. The Soul Calls
From Within Me: 'You, Ignorant Of The Way
Of Love, Set Me Free.'"
- Rumi

"My Fate Cannot Be Mastered; It Can Only Be Collaborated With And Thereby, To Some Extent, Directed. Nor Am I The Captain Of My Soul; I Am Only It Noisiest Passenger"
- Aldous Huxley

"Today I See Beauty Everywhere I Go, In Every Face I See, In Every Single Soul"
- Kevyn Aucoin

"Once Conform, Once Do What Others Do Because They Do It, And A Kind Of Lethargy Steals Over All Th Finer Senses Of The Soul"
- Michel De Montaigne

"I Was Thrown Out Of College For Cheating On The Metaphysics Exam: I Looked Into The Soul Of Another Boy" - Woody Allen

"Moderation Is The Feebleness And Sloth Of The Soul, Whereas Ambition Is The Warmth And Activity Of It"
- Francois De La Rochefoucauld

"I Have Often Thought With Wonder Of The Great Goodness Of God; And My Soul Has Rejoiced In The Contemplation Of His Great Magnificence And Mercy. May He Be Blessed For Ever! For I See Clearly That He Has Not Omitted To Reward Me, Even In This Life, For Every One Of My Good Desires"
- Saint Teresa Of Avila

"For As The Eyes Of Bats Are To The Blaze
Of Day, So Is The Reason In Our Soul
To The Things Which Are By Nature
Most Evident Of All" - Aristotle

"At Some Point You Will Realize Hard Time
Was The Best Part Of Your Life Because It
Is The Only Thing You Have To Test The Limit
Of Your Soul" - Unknown

"History Is Not A Burden On The Memory But
An Illumination Of The Soul" - Lord Acton

"Never Think There Is Anything Impossible For
The Soul. It Is The Greatest Heresy To Think
So. If There Is Sin, This Is The Only Sin; To
Say That You Are Weak, Or Others Are Weak"
- Swami Vivekananda

"I Might Have Some Character Traits That
Some Might See As Innocence Or Naive. That's
Because I Discovered Peace And Happiness In
My Soul. And With This Knowledge, I Also See
The Beauty Of Human Life"
- Tobey Maguire

"No One Ever Loses Anyone. We Are All One
Soul That Needs To Continue Growing And
Developing In Order For The World To Carry
On And For Us All To Meet Once Again"
- Unknown

"Every Secret Of A Writer's Soul, Every
Experience Of His Life, Every Quality Of
His Mind Is Written Large In His Works"
- Virginia Woolf

"No Iron Chain, Or Outward Force Of Any Kind,
Can Ever Compel The Soul Of A Person
To Believe Or To Disbelieve"
- Thomas Carlyle

"It Is My Own Firm Belief That The Strength
Of The Soul Grows In Proportion As You
Subdue The Flesh"
- Mahatma Gandhi

"I Love Cats Because I Enjoy My Home; And
Little By Little, They Become Its Visible Soul"
- Jean Cocteau

"The Cynicism That You Have Is Not
Your Real Soul" - Yoko Ono

"When You Start Fooling Around With Drugs,
You're Hurting Your Creativity, You're Hurting
Your Health. Drugs Are Death, In One Form
Or Another. If They Don't Kill You,
They Kill Your Soul. And If Your Soul's Dead,
You've Got Nothing To Offer, Anyway"
- Paul Stanley

"And For Me Anyway, Consciousness Is Three
Components: A Personal Component Which
For Lack Of A Better Word We Can Call The
Soul. A Collective Component Which Is More
Archetypal And A Deeper Level, And Then A
Universal Domain Of Consciousness"
- Deepak Chopra

"The Most Common Error Made In Matters
Of Appearance Is The Belief That One Should
Disdain The Superficial And Let The True
Beauty Of One's Soul Shine Through.
If There Are Places On Your Body Where
This Is A Possibility, You Are Not Attractive
- You Are Leaking" - Charles Lamb

"As Long As Your Body Is Healthy And Under
Control And Death Is Distant, Try To Save
Your Soul; When Death Is Immanent
What Can You Do" - Chanakya

"When You Do Things From Your Soul,
You Feel A River Moving In You, A Joy"
- Rumi

"No One Has Yet Realized The Wealth
Of Sympathy, The Kindness And Generosity
Hidden In The Soul Of A Child. The Effort Of
Every True Education Should Be To Unlock
That Treasure" - Emma Goldman

"The Soul, Touched By Divine Breathing,
Illuminates Consciousness That Enters
A Reality Beyond Worldly Things Inspiring
The Enlightened Spirit To Contemplate
And Act Upon What Can Be"
- Richard Marvin Voigt

"If God Gave The Soul His Whole Creation She
Would Not Be Filled Thereby But Only With
Himself" - Meister Eckhart

"The Great Question That Has Never Been
Answered, And Which I Have Not Yet Been
Able To Answer, Despite My Thirty Years
Of Research Into The Feminine Soul,
Is 'What Does A Woman Want?'"
- Sigmund Freud

"Everything That Is New Or Uncommon Raises
A Pleasure In The Imagination, Because It Fills
The Soul With An Agreeable Surprise, Gratifies
Its Curiosity, And Gives It An Idea Of Which
It Was Not Before Possessed."
- Joseph Addison

"Who Would Ever Think That So Much Went
On In The Soul Of A Young Girl "
- Anne Frank

"Nothing Can Cure The Soul But The Senses,
Just As Nothing Can Cure The Senses
But The Soul" - Oscar Wilde

"Egoism Is The Very Essence Of A Noble
Soul" - Friedrich Nietzsche

"For It Was Not Into My Ear You Whispered,
But Into My Heart. It Was Not My Lips You
Kissed, But My Soul" - Judy Garland

"I Simply Believe That Some Part Of The
Human Self Or Soul Is Not Subject To The
Laws Of Space And Time" - Carl Jung

"The Soul Becomes Dyed With The Color
Of Its Thoughts" - Marcus Aurelius

"Your Own Soul Is Nourished When You
Are Kind; It Is Destroyed When You Are Cruel"
- King Solomon

"Don't Do Anything By Half. If You Love
Someone, Love Them With All Your Soul..."
- Henry Rollins

"The Earth Has Grown Old With Its Burden Of
Care, But At Christmas It Always Is Young, The
Heart Of The Jewel Burns Lustrous And Fair, And
Its Soul Full Of Music Breaks The Air, When The
Song Of Angels Is Sung" - Phillips Brooks

"Hollywood Is A Place Where They'll Pay You A Thousand Dollars For A Kiss And Fifty Cents For Your Soul" - Marilyn Monroe

"I Have No Companion But Love, No Beginning, No End, No Dawn. The Soul Calls From Within Me: 'You, Ignorant Of The Way Of Love, Set Me Free'" - Rumi

"Your Soul Is Your Human Thread Residing Within The Ever-Expanding Fabric Of Universal Energy Adding Your Contribution To All That Was, Is, And Ever Will Be" - Richard Marvin Voigt

"It Matters Not How Strait The Gate, How Charged With Punishments The Scroll; I Am The Master Of My Fate: I Am The Captain Of My Soul" - William Ernest Henley

"Everywhere The Human Soul Stands Between A Hemisphere Of Light And Another Of Darkness; On The Confines Of The Two Everlasting Empires, Necessity And Free Will" - Thomas Carlyle

"It's A Long Road When You Face The World Alone, When No One Reaches Out A Hand For You To Hold. You Can Find Love If You Search Within Your Soul, And The Emptiness You Felt Will Disappear" - Mariah Carey

"A Home Without Books Is A Body
Without Soul" - Marcus Tullius Cicero

"If The Sight Of The Blue Skies Fills You With
Joy, If A Blade Of Grass Springing Up In The
Fields Has Power To Move You, If The Simple
Things Of Nature Have A Message That You
Understand, Rejoice, For Your Soul Is Alive"
- Eleonora Duse

"In A Free Society, Government Reflects The
Soul Of Its People. If People Want Change
At The Top, They Will Have To Live In Different
Ways. Our Major Social Problems Are Not
The Cause Of Our Decadence. They Are
A Reflection Of It" - Cal Thomas

"There Can Be No Keener Revelation Of
A Society's Soul That The Way In Which
It Treats Children" - Nelson Mandela

"In A Free Society, Government Reflects The
Soul Of Its People. If People Want Change
At The Top, They Will Have To Live In Different
Ways. Our Major Social Problems Are Not
The Cause Of Our Decadence. They Are
A Reflection Of It" - Cal Thomas

"Man Has Set For Himself The Goal Of Conquering The World But In The Processes Loses His Soul" - Aleksandr Solzhenitsyn

"If Having A Soul Means Being Able To Feel Love And Loyalty And Gratitude, Then Animal Are Better Off Than A Lot Of Human"
-   James Herriot

"Man Is So Made That When Anything Fires His Soul, Impossibilities Vanish"
- Jean De La Fontaine

"The Countenance Is The Portrait Of The Soul, And The Eyes Mark Its Intentions"
- Marcus Tullius Cicero

"Love Is When He Gives You A Piece Of Your Soul, That You Never Knew Was Missing"
- Torquato Tasso

"Beauty Of Whatever Kind, In Its Supreme Development, Invariably Excites The Sensitive Soul To Tears" - Edgar Allan Poe

"The Soul's Emphasis Is Always Right"
- Ralph Waldo Emerson

"There Is Nothing That Makes Its Way More Directly Into The Soul Than Beauty"
- Joseph Addison

"Life Beats Down And Crushes The Soul And
Art Reminds You That You Have One"
- Stella Adler

"We Must Not Tamper With The Organic Motion
Of The Soul" - Ralph Waldo Emerson

"God Is An Unutterable Sigh, Planted
In The Depths Of The Soul" - Jean Paul

"Hope Is The Struggle Of The Soul, Breaking
Loose From What Is Perishable, And Attesting
Her Eternity" - Herman Melville

"The Dogs Did Bark, The Children Screamed,
Up Flew The Windows All; And Every Soul
Bawled Out, Well Done! As Loud
As He Could Bawl" - William Cowper

"Never Had I Seen The Sun Shine
Brighter…Never Had I, Until The Day
You Touched My Soul With Your Love"
- Unknown

"That Is The Returning To God Which In Reality
Is Never Concluded On Earth But Yet Leaves
Behind In The Soul A Divine Home Sickness,
Which Never Again Ceases" - Max Muller

"As Long As Habit And Routine Dictate
The Pattern Of Living, New Dimensions Of
The Soul Will Not Emerge" - Henry Van Dyke

"Having A Life And Leadership Philosophy Is
Essential For Living In An Inspired Way And
Leading With Soul And Spirit" - Senora Ray

"Nations, Like Stars, Are Entitled To Eclipse.
All Is Well, Provided The Light Returns And
The Eclipse Does Not Become Endless Night.
Dawn And Resurrection Are Synonymous.
The Reappearance Of The Light Is The Same
As The Survival Of The Soul." - Victor Hugo

"You Know Why We're Stuck With The Myth
That Only Black People Have Soul?
Because White People Don't Let Themselves
Feel Things" - Janis Joplin

"Divine Providence... Keeps The Universe
Open In Every Direction To The Soul..."
- Ralph Waldo Emerson

"A Consistent Soul Believes In Destiny,
A Capricious One In Chance"
- Benjamin Disraeli

"Stop Chasing What Your Mind Wants And
You'll Get What Your Soul Needs" - Unknown

"Let Your Mind Start A Journey Through A
Strange New World. Leave All Thoughts Of
The World You Knew Before. Let Your Soul
Take You Where You Long To Be…Close Your
Eyes Let Your Spirit Start To Soar, And You'll
Live As You've Never Lived Before"
-   Erich Fromm

"The Most Powerful Weapon On Earth
Is The Human Soul On Fire" - Ferdinand Foch

"Each Religion, By The Help Of More Or Less
Myth, Which It Takes More Or Less Seriously,
Proposes Some Method Of Fortifying
The Human Soul And Enabling It
To Make Its Peace With Its Destiny"
-   George Santayana

"Let Us Dream Of Tomorrow Where We Can
Truly Love From The Soul, And Know Love
As The Ultimate Truth At The Heart
Of All Creation" - Michael Jackson

"A Healthy Social Life Is Found Only, When In
The Mirror Of Each Soul The Whole
Community Finds Its Reflection, And When In
The Whole Community The Virtue Of Each One
Is Living" - Rudolf Steiner

"Dreams Nourish The Soul Just As Food
Nourishes The Body. The Pleasure Of The
Search And Of Adventure Feeds Our Dreams"
- Unknown

"Poverty Of Goods Is Easily Cured; Poverty Of
Soul, Impossible" - Michel De Montaigne

"To Deprive A Man Of His Natural Liberty And
To Deny Him The Ordinary Amenities Of Live Is
Worse Than Starving The Body; It Is Starvation
Of The Soul, The Dweller In The Body"
- Mahatma Gandhi

"Truth Adds Strength To Our Mind, Courage
To Our Heart, Happiness To Our Soul And
Empowerment, Motivation And Inspiration
To Feel The Best In Our Enriching Life"
- Ritu Ghatourey

"In Your Lifetime You Will Meet One Person
Who Is Unlike Any Other, You Can Tell Them
Any And Everything And They Won't Judge
You...This Person Is You Soul-Mate,
Your Best Friend...Don't Ever Let Them Go"
- Rashida Rowe

"Dance Is The Hidden Language Of The Soul
Of The Body" - Martha Graham

"The Soul That Is Within Me No Man Can
Degrade" - Frederick Douglas

"It Would Be Idle To Say That Life Is A Steady
Progression In Happiness. But It Is Most
Certain That In The Natural Course Of Things
A Healthy Soul Grows Continually Richer Until
Its Latest Day On Earth" - George S. Merriam

"One May Have A Blazing Hearth In One's Soul
And Yet No One Ever Come To Sit By It.
Passers-By See Only A Wisp Of Smoke From
The Chimney And Continue On The Way"
- Vincent Van Gogh

"I Do Not Believe In Political Movements.
I Believe In Personal Movement, That
Movement Of The Soul When A Man
Who Looks At Himself Is So Ashamed
That He Tries To Make Some Sort Of Change
- Within Himself, Not On The Outside"
- Joseph Brodsky

"Life Delivered Me A Catastrophe, But I Found
A Richness Of Soul" - Michael J. Fox

"Who Can Map Out The Various Forces At Play
In One Soul? Man Is A Great Depth, O Lord.
The Hairs Of His Head Are Easier By Far
To Count Than His Feeling, The Movements
Of His Heart" - Saint Augustine

"Curiosity, N. An Objectionable Quality Of The Female Mind. The Desire To Know Whether Or Not A Woman Is Cursed With Curiosity Is One Of The Most Active And Insatiable Passions Of The Masculine Soul"
- Ambrose Bierce

"While The Soul Is In Mortal Sin, Nothing Can Profit It; None Of Its Good Works Merit An Eternal Reward, Since They Do Not Proceed From God As Their First Principle, And By Him Alone Is Our Virtue Real Virtue"
- Saint Teresa Of Avila

"If You Die You're Completely Happy And Your Soul Somewhere Lives On. I'm Not Afraid Of Dying. Total Peace After Death, Becoming Someone Else Is The Best Hope I've Got"
- Kurt Cobain

"In A State Of Grace, The Soul Is Like A Well Of Limpid Water, From Which Flow Only Streams Of Clearest Crystal. Its Works Are Pleasing Both To God And Man, Rising From The River Of Life, Beside Which It Is Rooted Like A Tree" - Saint Teresa Of Avila

"Put Your Heart, Mind, And Soul Into Even Your Smallest Acts. This Is The Secret Of Success"
- Swami Sivananda

"Were I Called On To Define Very Briefly,
The Term Art, I Should Call It The Reproduction
Of What The Senses Perceive In Nature
Thought The Veil Of The Soul…"
- Edgar Allan Poe

"I've Come To Trust Not That Events Will
Always Unfold Exactly As I Want, But That I Will
Be Fine Either Way. The Challenges We Face
In Life Are Always Lessons That Serve
Our Soul's Growth" - Marianne Williamson

"The Memory Of My Own Suffering Has
Prevented Me From Ever Shadowing One
Young Soul With The Superstition Of The
Christian Religion" - Elizabeth Cady Stanton

"Character Cannot Be Developed In Ease
And Quiet. Only Through Experience Of Trial
And Suffering Can The Soul Be Strengthened,
Ambition Inspired, And Success Achieved"
- Helen Keller

"What Then Do You Call Your Soul? What Idea
Have You Of It? You Cannot Of Yourselves,
Without Revelation, Admit The Existence Within
You Of Anything But A Power Unknown To You
Of Feeling And Thinking" - Voltaire

"Those Things That Nature Denied To Human Sight, She Revealed To The Eyes Of The Soul" - Ovid

"Alas! All Music Jars When The Soul's Out Of Tune" - Miguel De Cervantes

"Friendship Is Composed Of A Single Soul Inhabiting Two Bodies" - Plautus

"There Can Be A True Grandeur In Any Degree Of Submissiveness, Because It Springs From Loyalty To The Laws And To An Oath, And Not From Baseness Of Soul" - Simone Weil

"There's Nothing Like Music To Relieve The Soul And Uplift It" - Mickey Hart

"Why Do You Hasten To Remove Anything Which Hurts Your Eye, While If Something Affects Your Soul You Postpone The Cure Until Next Year" - Horace

"Whether If Soul Did Not Exist, Time Would Exist Or Not, Is A Question That May Fairly Be Asked; For It There Cannot Be Someone To Count There Cannot Be Anything That Can Be Counted, So That Evidently There Cannot Be Number; For Number Is Either What Has Been, Or What Can Be Counted" - Aristotle

"The Soul Is Healed By Being With Children"
- Fyodor Dostoyevsky

"Health Is The Soul That Animates All The
Enjoyments Of Life, Which Fade And Are
Tasteless Without It" - Lucius Annaeus Seneca

"Thinking: The Talking Of The Soul With Itself"
- Plato

"When The Soul, Through Its Own Fault...
Becomes Rooted In A Pool Of Pitch-Black,
Evil Smelling Water, It Produces Nothing But
Misery And Filth" - Saint Teresa Of Avila

"Never Does The Human Soul Appear
So Strong As When It Foregoes Revenge
And Dares To Forgive An Injury"
- Edwin Hubbel Chapin

"The Soul Is So Far From Being A Monad That
We Have Not Only To Interpret Other Souls To
Ourself But To Interpret Ourself To Ourself"
- T. S. Eliot

"Certain Thoughts Are Prayers. There Are
Moments When, Whatever Be The Attitude
Of The Body, The Soul Is On Its Knees"
- Victor Hugo

"It Takes More Than Just A Good Looking Body. You've Got To Have The Heart And Soul To Go With It" - Epcitetus

"The Mother Art Is Architecture. Without An Architecture Of Our Own We Have No Soul Of Our Own Civilization" - Frank Lloyd Wright

"Charms Strike The Sight, But Merit Wins The Soul" - Alexander Pope

"A Wretched Soul, Bruised With Adversity, We Bid Be Quiet When We Hear It Cry; But Were We Burdened With Like Weight Of Pain, As Much Or More We Should Ourselves Complain" - William Shakespeare

"To Me, It Seems A Dreadful Indignity To Have A Soul Controlled By Geography" - George Santayana

"The Artist Produces For The Liberation Of His Soul. It Is His Nature To Create As It Is The Nature Of Water To Run Down The Hill" - W. Somerset Maugham

"You Start Out Giving Your Hat, Then You Give Your Coat, Then Your Shirt, Then Your Skin And Finally Your Soul" - Charles De Gaulle

"Care I For The Limb, The Thews, The Stature,
Bulk, And Big Assemblance Of A Man!
Give Me The Spirit" - William Shakespeare

"You Use A Glass Mirror To See Your Face;
You Use Works Of Art To See Your Soul"
- George Bernard Shaw

-

"In A Mirror We Find A Reflection Of Our
Appearances, But In Heart We Find
A Reflection Of Soul" - Unknown

"Take A Moment Each Day To Let The Beauty
Of Your Life Grasp Hold Of Your Soul
And Be Able To Lose Yourself In How Lucky
You Really Are" - Senora Ray

"Astronomy Compels The Soul To Look
Upwards And Lead Us From This World
To Another" - Plato

"I'm Not Claiming Divinity. I've Never Claimed
Purity Of Soul. I've Never Claimed To Have
The Answers To Life. I Only Put Out Songs
And Answer Questions As Honestly As
I Can...But I Still Believe In Peace, Love And
Understanding" - John Lennon

"What Difference Is There Between Us, Save
A Restless Dream That Follows My Soul But
Fears To Come Near You" - Khalil Gibran

"Time Always Seems Long To The Child Who Is Waiting - For Christmas, For Next Summer, For Becoming A Grownup: Long Also When He Surrenders His Whole Soul To Each Moment Of A Happy Day" - Dag Hammarskjold

"The Science Of The Mind Can Only Have For Its Proper Goal The Understanding Of Human Nature By Every Human Being, And Through Its Use, Brings Peace To Every Human Soul"
- Alfred Adler

"Souls Wouldn't Wear Suits And Ties, They'd Wear Blue Jeans And Sit Cross-Legged With A Glass Of Red Wine" - Terri Guillemets

"Originality Is The Essence Of True Scholarship. Creativity Is The Soul Of The True Scholar" - Nnamdi Azikiwe

"The Face Is The Soul Of The Body"
- Ludwig Wittgenstein

"Until You Know That Life Is Interesting – And Find It So - You Haven't Found Your Soul"
- Goeffrey Fisher

"I Think That A Lot Of Us, Whether We Are Religious Or Not - There Are No Words To Express Some Things Except Religious Words. For Instance, 'Soul'" - Salman Rushdie

"The Danger Is Not Lest The Soul Should Doubt Whether There Is Any Bread, But Lest, By A Lie, It Should Persuade Itself That It Is Not Hungry." - Simone Weil

"You Have To Grow From The Inside Out. None Can Teach You, None Can Make You Spiritual. There Is No Other Teacher But Your Own Soul" - Swami Vivekananda

"Independence? That's Middle Class Blasphemy. We Are All Dependent On One Another, Every Soul Of Us On Earth" - George Bernard Shaw

"Whoso Will Pray, He Must Fast And Be Clean, And Fat His Soul, And Make His Body Lean" - Geoffrey Chaucer

"What He Had Yearned To Embrace Was Not The Flesh But A Downy Spirit, A Spark, The Impalpable Angel That Inhabits The Flesh" - Antoine De Saint-Exupery

"Your Soul Is A Dark Forest. But The Trees Are Of A Particular Species, They Are Genealogical Trees" - Marcel Proust

"In These Times, God's People Must Trust Him For Rest Of Body And Soul" - David Wilkerson

"Listen! Clam Up Your Mouth And Be Silent
Like An Oyster Shell, For That Tongue Of
Yours Is The Enemy Of The Soul, My Friend.
When The Lips Are Silent, The Heart Has
A Hundred Tongues" - Rumi

"Be Good, Keep Your Feet Dry, Your Eyes
Open, Your Heart At Peace And Your Soul
In The Joy Of Christ" - Thomas Merton

"Spiritual Relationship Is Far More Precious
Than Physical. Physical Relationship Divorced
From Spiritual Is Body Without Soul"
- Mahatma Gandhi

"Solitude Terrifies The Soul At Twenty"
- Moliere

"One Who Sees The Supersoul Accompanying
The Individual Soul In All Bodies And Who
Understands That Neither The Soul Nor The
Supersoul Is Ever Destroyed, Actually Sees"
- Marcus Tullius Cicero

"The First Thing Which I Can Record
Concerning Myself Is, That I Was Born.
They Are Wonderful Words. This Life,
To Which Neither Time Not Eternity Can
Bring Diminution - This Everlasting Living Soul,
Began. My Mind Loses Itself In These Depths"
- Groucho Marx

"Prayer Is Not Asking. It Is A Longing Of The Soul. It Is Daily Admission Of One's Weakness. It Is Better In Prayer To Have A Heart Without Words Than Words Without A Heart" - Mahatma Gandhi

"There Are Victories Of The Soul And Spirit. Sometimes, Even If You Lose, You Win"
- Elie Wiesel

"We Had Seen God In His Splendors, Heard The Text That Nature Renders. We Had Reached The Naked Soul Of Man"
- Ernest Shackleton

"Love Is A Portion Of The Soul Itself, And It Is Of The Same Nature As The Celestial Breathing Of The Atmosphere Of Paradise"
- Victor Hugo

"Living Is Being Born Slowly. It Would Be A Little Too Easy If We Could Borrow Ready-Made Souls"
- Antoine De Saint-Exupery

"Love To His Soul Gave Eyes; He Knew Things Are Not As They Seem. The Dream Is His Real Life; Te World Around Him Is The Dream"
- Michel De Montaigne

"Brevity Is The Soul Of Wit"
- William Shakespeare

"We Must Go Beyond The Constant Clamor
Of Ego, Beyond The Tools Of Logic And
Reason, To The Still, Calm Place Within Us:
The Realm Of The Soul" - Deepak Chopra

"Loyalty To Petrified Opinion Never Yet Broke A
Chain Or Freed A Human Soul" - Mark Twain

"The Love Of Husband And Wife, Which Is
Creative Of New Human Life, Is A Marvellously
Personal Sharing In The Creative Love Of God
Who Brings Into Being The Eternal Soul That
Comes To Every Human Being With The Gift
Of Human Life" - Vincent Nichols

"One Certainly Has A Soul; But How It Came
To Allow Itself To Be Enclosed In A Body
Is More Than I Can Imagine. I Only Know If
Once Mine Gets Out, I'll Have A Bit Of A Tussle
Before I Let It Get In Again To That
Of Any Other" - Lord Byron

"It Is Great Wealth To A Soul To Live Frugally
With A Contented Mind" - Lucretius

"Earth Changes, But Thy Soul And God
Stand Sure" - Robert Browning

"True Religion Is Real Living; Living With All One's Soul, With All One's Goodness And Righteousness" - Albert Einstein

"Whenever Anyone Has Offended Me, I Try To Raise My Soul So High That The Offense Cannot Reach It" - Rene Descartes

"Peace Is Not A Relationship Of Nations. It Is A Condition Of Mind Brought About By A Serenity Of Soul. Peace Is Not Merely The Absence Of War. It Is Also A State Of Mind. Lasting Peace Can Come Only To Peaceful People"
- Jawaharial Nehru

"Try To Keep Your Soul Young And Quivering Right Up To Old Age" - George Sand

"America Took Me Into Her Bosom When There Was No Longer A Country Worthy Of The Name, But In My Heart I Am German - German In My Soul" - Marlene Dietrich

"I Grow Plants For Many Reasons: To Please My Eye Or To Please My Soul, To Challenge The Elements Or To Challenge My Patience, For Novelty Or For Nostalgia, But Mostly For The Joy In Seeing Them Grow"
- David Hobson

"To Buy Happiness Is To Sell Soul"
- Douglas Horton

"Our Storyboard Of Life Is Often Characterized
By Images Of Nouns Until We Elect To Animate
Them By The Action Verbs Of Our Soul"
- Richard Marvin Voigt

"What Friends Or Kindred Can Be So Close
And Intimate As The Powers Of Our Soul,
Which, Whether We Will Or No, Must Ever Bear
Us Company" - Saint Teresa Of Avila

"Free Will Carried Many A Soul To Hell, But
Never A Soul To Heaven" - Charles Spurgeon

"People Know About The Klan And The Overt
Racism, But The Killing Of One's Soul Little
By Little, Day After Day, Is A Lot Worse
Than Someone Coming In Your House
And Lynching You" - Omar Khayyam

"Yes, Now I Understood For The First Time
That My Soul Was Not So Poor And Empty As
It Had Seemed To Me, And That It Had Been
Only The Sun That Was Lacking To Open All
Its Germs, And Buds To The Light"
- Max Muller

"A Bad Book Is As Much Of A Labor To Write
As A Good One, It Comes As Sincerely From
The Author's Soul" - Aldous Huxley

"A Man At Work, Making Something Which
He Feels Will Exist Because He Is Working
At It And Wills It, Is Exercising The Energies
Of His Mind And Soul As Well As Of His Body.
Memory And Imagination Help Him
As He Works" - William Morris

"Freedom Is The Oxygen Of The Soul"
- Moshe Dayan

"Forests, Lakes, And Rivers, Clouds And
Winds, Stars And Flowers, Stupendous
Glaciers And Crystal Snowflakes - Every Form
Of Animate Or Inanimate Existence, Leaves Its
Impress Upon The Soul Of Man"
- Orison Swett Marden

"I Think We're Going To The Moon Because
It's In The Nature Of The Human Being To
Face Challenges. It's By The Nature Of His
Deep Inner Soul... We're Required To Do
These Things Just As Salmon Swim
Upstream" - Neil Armstrong

"Until One Has Loved An Animal, A Part Of
One's Soul Remains Unwakened"
- Anatole France

"Music Is The Soul That Can Be Heard
By The Universe" - Lao Tzu

"I Write From My Soul. This Is The Reason
That Critics Don't Hurt Me, Because It Is Me.
If It Was Not Me, If I Was Pretending To Be
Someone Else, Then This Could Unbalance My
World, Bu I Know Who I Am" - Paulo Coelho

"No Matter How Difficult And Painful It May Be,
Nothing Sounds As Good To The Soul
As The Truth" - Martha Beck

"It's Usually A Big Kind Of Vent Of Frustration
Or Anger Or Sadness That Puts Me In The
Right Frame Of Mind To Write. It's Such A
Cliche To Say That Artists Write When They're
Down, But It's True For Me. It's A Relief To Get
Out What's Eating Away At My Heart Or My
Soul Or My Head" - Ellie Goulding

"I'm Not A Fighter, But In My Mind I'm Fighting
Every Day. 'What's New? What Am I Doing?'
I'm Fighting Myself. My Soul Is Samurai.
My Roots Aren't Samurai, But My Soul Is"
- Masaharu Morimoto

"No Matter How Difficult And Painful It May Be,
Nothing Sounds As Good To The Soul
As The Truth" - Martha Beck

"Friendship, Like The Immortality Of The Soul,
Is Too Good To Be Believed"
- Ralph Waldo Emerson

"Put Your Ear Down Close To Your Soul
And Listen Hard" - Anne Sexton

"The Essence Of True Education In One's Life
Is To Show Presence Of Mind, Heart And Soul
To Sense Everything Right" - Anuj Somany

"The Universal Medicine For The Soul Is The
Supreme Reason And Absolute Justice;
For The Mind, Mathematical And Practical
Truth; For The Body, The Quintessence,
A Combination Of Light And Gold"
- Albert Pike

"Since Love Grows Within You, So Beauty
Grows. For Love Is The Beauty Of The Soul"
- Saint Augustine

"Youth Is The Period In Which A Man Can Be
Hopeless. The End Of Every Episode Is The
End Of The World. But The Power Of Hoping
Through Everything, The Knowledge That The
Soul Survives Its Adventures, That Great
Inspiration Comes To The Middle-Aged"
- Gilbert K. Chesterton

"Every Production Of An Artist Should Be The Expression Of An Adventure Of His Soul"
- W. Somerset Maugham

"I Said To My Soul, Be Still, And Wait Without Hope. For Hope Would Be Hope
For The Wrong Thing" - T. S. Eliot

"Paintings Have A Life Of Their Own That Derives From The Painter's Soul"
- Vincent Van Gogh

"From Seeds Of His Body Blossomed The Flower That Liberated A People And Touched The Soul Of A Nation" - Jesse Jackson

"To Know How To Suggest Is The Great Art Of Teaching. To Attain It We Must Be Able To Guess What Will Interest; We Must Learn To Read The Childish Soul As We Might A Piece Of Music. Then, By Simply Changing The Key, We Keep Up The Attraction And Vary The Song" - Henri Frederic Amiel

"The Soul That See Beauty May Sometimes Walk Alone" - Johann Wolfgan vom Goethe

"There Is Something About Killing People At Close Range That Is Excruciating. It's Bound To Try A Man's Soul" - Steven Spielberg

"Seeing My Malevolent Face In The Mirror, My
Benevolent Soul Shrinks Back"
- Mason Cooley

"Be Careless In Your Dress If You Must,
But Keep A Tidy Soul" - Mark Twain
"He That Has Light Within His Own Clear
Breast May Sit In The Centre, And Enjoy Bright
Day: But He That Hides A Dark Soul And Foul
Thoughts Benighted Walks Under The Mid-Day
Sun; Himself His Own Dungeon" - John Milton

"I Put My Heart And Soul Into My Work, And
Have Lost My Mind In The Process"
- Vincent Van Gogh

"What Is Success? It Is Being Able To Go To
Bed Each Night With Your Soul At Peace"
- Paulo Coelho

"You Don't Have A Soul. You Are A Soul. You
Have A Body" - Walter M. Miller Jr.

"I Am A Real Person That Cares About His Art
And Cares About What He's Doing - I Have A
Heart And A Soul And Want To Touch People
And Give" - LL Cool J

"Things Won Are Done, Joy's Soul Lies In
The Doing" - William Shakespeare

"Ambition Is A Dead Sea Fruit, And The
Greatest Peril To The Soul Is That One Is
Likely To Get Precisely What He Is Seeking"
- Edward Dahlberg

"Every Moment And Every Event Of Every
Man's Life On Earth Plants Something
In His Soul" - Thomas Merton

"Where Is Your Soul You Ask? It Dwells Deep
Within One's Equity Core Where Access To
The Expansion Of Untapped Universal Energy
Resides" - Richard Marvin Voigt

"The Man Who Is Always Worrying About
Whether Or Not His Soul Would Be Damned
Generally Has A Soul That Isn't Worth A
Damn" - Oliver Wendell Holmes, Sr.

"An Election Is A Moral Horror, As Bas As A
Battle Except For The Blood; A Mud Bath For
Every Soul Concerned In It"
- George Bernard Shaw

"Each Soul Shares Responsibility In Expanding
Mankind's Collective Equity Whereby The Laws
Of Universal Energy Infinitely Expands
Uncharted Infinities" - Richard Marvin Voigt

"Humility Is The Foundation Of All The Other Virtues Hence, In The Soul In Which This Virtue Does Not Exist There Cannot Be Any Other Virtue Except In Mere Appearance"
- Saint Augustine

"A Sensible Man Will Remember That The Eyes May Be Confused In Two Ways - By A Change From Light To Darkness Or From Darkness To Light; And He Will Recognize That The Same Thing Happens To The Soul" - Plato

"Those Who Gave Thee A Body, Furnished It With Weakness; But He Who Gave Thee Soul, Armed Thee With Resolution. Employ It, And Thou Art Wise; Be Wise And Thou Art Happy"
- Akhenaton

"Happiness Resides Not In Possessions, And Not In Gold, Happiness Dwells In The Soul"
- Democritus

"Rude Contact With Facts Chased My Visions And Dreams Quickly Away, And In Their Stead I Beheld The Horrors, The Corruption, The Evils And Hypocrisy Of Society, And As I Stood Among Them, A Young Wife, A Great Wail Of Agony Went Out From My Soul"
- Victoria Woodhull

"A Man Sooner Or Later Discovers That He Is The Master-Gardener Of His Soul, The Director Of His Life" - James Allen

"An Aged Man Is But A Paltry Thing, A Tattered Coat Upon A Stick, Unless Soul Clap Its Hands And Sing, And Louder Sing For Every Tatter In Its Mortal Dress" - William Butler Yeats

"I Thought Of The Soul As Resembling A Castle, Formed Of A Single Diamond Or A Very Transparent Crystal, And Containing Many Rooms, Just As In Heaven There Are Many Mansions" - Saint Teresa Of Avila

"Faith Doesn't Come From Your Heart Or Mind, It Comes From Your Soul. It Is A Spiritual Force. It Is The Assurance Of Things Hoped For, The Conviction Of Things Not Seen" - Glen Rambharack

"You Know The Value Of Every Article Of Merchandise, But If You Don't Know The Value Of Your Own Soul, It's All Foolishness" - Rumi

"Cherish Your Visions And Your Dreams As The Are The Children Of You Soul, The Blue-prints Of Your Ultimate Achievements" - Napoleon Hill

"A Puny Body Weakens The Soul"
- Paul Cezanne

"Anticipation Awakes The Passion, Vision
Ignites The Heart, Touch Erupts The Soul"
- Craig D. Slovak

"A Beginner Must Look On Himself As One
Setting Out To Make A Garden For His Lord's
Pleasure, On Most Unfruitful Soil Which
Abounds In Weeds. His Majesty Roots Up The
Weeds And Will Put In Good Plants Instead.
Let Us Reckon That This Is Already Done
When The Soul Decides To Practice Prayer
And Has Begun To Do So"
- Saint Teresa Of Avila

"Early On In My Life, I Had A Broken Soul.
I Was Abused By My Father, Abandoned By My
Mother And Ended Up In A Destructive First
Marriage. By The Time I Was 23, I Was Broken
In My Soul. I Didn't Know How To Think Right. I
Felt Wrong About Everything. But God Stepped
Into My Life, And I Came Out On The Other
Side And Didn't Even Smell Like Smoke"
- Joyce Meyer

"Once In A Lifetime, You'll Find A Friend Who
Touches Not Only Your Heart, But Your Soul"
- Unknown

"These Are The Soul's Changes. I Don't Believe
In Ageing. I Believe In Forever Altering One's
Aspect To The Sun. Hence My Optimism"
- Virginia Woolf

"All Great Art Is The Work Of The Whole
Living Creature, Body And Soul, And Chiefly
Of The Soul" - John Ruskin

"You Are A Little Soul Carrying Around
A Corpse." - Epictetus

"In Books Lies The Soul Of The Whole
Past Time" - Thomas Carlyle

"I Have Found That Among Its Other Benefits,
Giving Liberates The Soul Of The Giver"
- May Angelou

"As A Body Everyone Is Single, As A Soul
Never" - Hermann Hesse

"You've Got To Show Your Soul Otherwise
You're Just A Piece Of Equipment"
- Sylvester Stallone

"Education Is Simply The Soul Of A Society As
It Passes From One Generation To Another"
- Gilbert K. Chesterton

"If I Am Elected President Of These United States, I Will Work With All My Energy And Soul To Restore That America, To Lift Our Eyes To A Better Future. That Future Is Our Destiny. That Future Is Out There. It Is Waiting For Us. Our Children Deserve It, Our Nation Depends Upon It, The Peace And Freedom Of The World Require It" - Mitt Romney

"When One Tears Away The Veils And Shows Them Naked, People's Souls Give Off Such A Pungent Smell Of Decay" - Octave Mirbeau

"Life Ought To Be A Struggle Of Desire Toward Adventures Whose Nobility Will Fertilize The Soul" - Rebecca West

"Style Is As Much Under The Words As In The Words. It Is As Much The Soul As It Is The Flesh Of A Work" - Gustave Flaubert

"Only One Who Devotes Himself To A Cause With His Whole Strength And Soul Can Be A True Master. For The Reason Mastery Demands All Of A Person"
- Albert Einstein

"Whatever Satisfies The Soul Is Truth"
- Walt Whitman

"Here Is The Deepest Secret Nobody Knows.
Here Is The Root Of The Root And The Bud
Of The Bud And The Sky Of The Sky Of A Tree
Called Life; Which Grows Higher That Soul Can
Hope Or Mind Can Hide. And This Is The
Wonder That's Keeping The Stars Apart.
I Carry You Heart. I Carry Your Heart"
- E E Cummings

"Your Soul Is The Culmination Of Every
Chosen Thought, Feeling And Action Taken
And Is Now The Reflective Spirit Of Who You
Are As Of This Very Moment In Time"
- Richard Marvin Voigt

"The Eyes Of The Soul Of The Multitudes Are
Unable To Endure The Vision Of The Divine"
- Plato

"The Soul Has Illusions As The Bird Has Wings:
It Is Supported By Them" - Victor Hugo

"The Beauty Of A Woman Is Not In A Facial
Mode But The True Beauty Of A Woman Is
Reflected In Her Soul. It Is The Caring That
She Lovingly Gives The Passions That She
Shows. The Beauty Of A Woman Grows With
The Passing Years" - Audrey Hepburn

"Greed Has Taken The Whole Universe, And
Nobody Is Worried About Their Soul"
- Little Richard

"My Records Are Borderline Dance Records.
They've Got A Real Electro-Rock Heart And
Soul, And The Vibe Of The Sentiment Is Pop,
But There's A Lot Of People That Were Like,
'This Is A Dance Record'" - Lady Gaga

"The Soul Is The Voice Of The Body's
Interests" - George Santayana

"I Am A Soul. I Know Well That What I Shall
Render Up To The Grave Is Not Myself. That
Which Is Myself Will Go Elsewhere. Earth,
Thou Art Not My Abyss" - Victor Hugo

"The Soul Can Split The Sky In Two And Let
The Face Of God Shine Through"
- Edna St. Vincent Millay

"It's So Clear That You Have To Cherish
Everyone. I Think That's What I Get From
These Older Black Women, That Every Soul Is
To Be Cherished, That Every Flower Is
To Bloom" - Alice Walker

"To Be Rooted Is Perhaps The Most Important
And Least Recognized Need Of
The Human Soul" - Simone Well

"I Think The Most Important Thing In Life Is Self-Love, Because If You Don't Have Self-Love, And Respect For Everything About Your Own Body, Your Own Soul, Your Own Capsule, Then How Can You Have An Authentic Relationship With Anyone Else"
- Shailene Woodley

"To Be Rooted Is Perhaps The Most Important And Least Recognized Need Of The Human Soul" - Simone Well

"I Think The Most Important Thing In Life Is Self-Love, Because If You Don't Have Self-Love, And Respect For Everything About Your Own Body, Your Own Soul, Your Own Capsule, Then How Can You Have An Authentic Relationship With Anyone Else"
- Shailene Woodley

"The Greatest Achievement Was At First And For A Time A Dream. The Oak Sleeps In The Acorn, The Bird Waits In The Egg, And In The Highest Vision Of The Soul A Waking Angel Stirs. Dreams Are The Seedlings Of Realities"
- James Allen

"God's Presence Is A Life Preserver That Keeps The Soul From Sinking In A Sea Of Trouble" - Unknown

"Soul Meets Soul On Lovers' Lips"
- Percy Bysshe Shelley

"The Soul Without Imagination Is What An
Observatory Would Be Without A Telescope"
- Henry Ward Beecher

"Love To His Soul Gave Eyes; He Knew Things
Are Not As They Seem. The Dream Is His Real
Life; The World Around Him Is The Dream"
-   Michel De Montaigne

"Wisdom Is To The Soul What Health Is
To The Body" - Unknown

"Power Always Thinks It Has A Great Soul And
Vast Views Beyond The Comprehension Of
The Weak" - John Adams

"Nobody Grows Old Merely By Living A Number
Of Years. We Grow Old By Deserting Our
Ideals. Years May Wrinkle The Skin, But
To Give Up Enthusiasm Wrinkles The Soul"
- Samuel Ullman

"The Soul, Which Is Spirit, Can Not Dwell In
Dust; It Is Carried Along To Dwell In The
Blood" - Saint Augustine

"Food For The Body Is Not Enough. There Must Be Food For The Soul" - Dorothy Day

"Enthusiasm Is The Energy And Force That Builds Literal Momentum Of The Human Soul And Mind" - Bryant H. Mcgill

"But If Nothing But Soul, Or In Soul Mind, Is Qualified To Count, It Is Impossible For There To Be Time Unless There Is Soul, But Only That Of Which Time Is An Attribute, i.e. If Change Can Exist Without Soul" - Aristotle

"The History Of Progress Is Written In The Blood Of Men And Women Who Have Dared To Espouse An Unpopular Cause, As, For Instance, The Black Man's Right To His Body, Or Woman's Right To Her Soul"
- Emma Goldman

"Character Is Higher Than Intellect. A Great Soul Will Be Strong And Live As Well As Think" - Ralph Waldo Emerson

"He Must Pull Out His Own Eyes, And See No Creature, Before He Can Say, He Sees No God; He Must Be No Man, And Quench His Reasonable Soul, Before He Can Say To Himself, There Is No God" - John Donne

"In Life, The Best Love Is The Kind That
Awaken The Soul And We Have No Doubts,
The Kind Of Love That Plants A Fire In Our
Hearts That Never Goes Out" - Rashida Rowe

"The Beauty That Addresses Itself To The Eyes
Is Only The Spell Of The Moment; The Eye Of
The Body Is Not Always That Of The Soul"
- George Sand

"There Is Not A Soul Who Does Not Have To
Beg Alms Of Another, Either A Smile, A
Handshake, Or A Fond Eye" - Lord Acton

"A Soul Is But The Last Bubble Of A Long
Fermentation In The World"
- George Santayana

"God Is Not Present In Idols. Your Feelings Are
Your God. The Soul Is Your Temple"
- Chanakya

"The Best Richness Is The Richness
Of The Soul" - Prophet Mohammed

"Only Passions, Great Passions Can Elevate
The Soul To Great Things" - Denis Diderot

"Meditation Is The Tongue Of The Soul
And The Language Of Our Spirit"
- Jeremy Taylor

"One Of My Proudest Moments Is I
Didn't Sell My Soul For The Sake
Of Popularity" - George W. Bush

"You See What Kills Your Body But You Don't
See What Kills Your Soul" - Lacey Mosley

"Knowledge Is The Eye Of Desire And Can
Become The Pilot Of The Soul" - Will Durant

"The Greatest Thing A Human Soul Ever Does
In This World... To See Clearly Is Poetry,
Prophecy And Religion All In One"
- John Ruskin

"Delicious Autumn! My Very Soul Is Wedded
To It, And If I Were A Bird I Would Fly About
The Earth Seeking The Successive Autumns"
- George Eliot

"You See, When Weaving A Blanket, An Indian
Woman Leaves A Flaw In The Weaving Of That
Blanket To Let The Soul Out"
- Martha Graham

"For What Shall It Profit A Man, If He Gain
The Whole World, And Suffer The Loss
Of His Soul" - Jesus Christ

"Permanence, Perseverance And Persistence In Spite Of All Obstacles, Discouragements, And Impossibilities: It Is This, That In All Things Distinguishes The Strong Soul From The Weak" - Thomas Carlyle

"How Good Is Man's Life, The Mere Living! How Fit To Employ All The Heart And The Soul And The Senses Forever In Joy"
- Robert Browning

"The Immortality Of The Soul Is A Matter Which Is Of So Great Consequence To Us And Which Touches Us So Profoundly That We Must Have Lost All Feeling To Be Indifferent About It"
- Blaise Pascal

"Cancer Can Take Away All Of My Physical Abilities. It Cannot Touch My Mind, It Cannot Touch My Heart, And It Cannot Touch My Soul" - Jim Valvano

"I Count Life Just A Stuff To Try The Soul's Strength On" - Robert Browning

"You Are The Only Person Alive Who Had Sole Custody Of Your Life…Your Entire Life…Not Just The Life Of Your Mind, But The Life Of Your Heart. Not Just Your Bank Account, But Your Soul" - Anna Quindlen

"Buddhism Has A Very Beautiful Teaching That Says The Worst Thing You Can Do To Your Soul Is To Tell Someone Their Faith Is Wrong" - Ricky Martin

"If The Grandfather Of The Grandfather Of Jesus Had Known What Was Hidden Within Him, He Would Have Stood Humble And Awestruck Before His Soul" - Khalil Gibran

"There Is A Serene And Settled Majesty To Woodland Scenery That Enters Into The Soul And Delights And Elevates It, And Fills It With Noble Inclinations" - Washington Irving

"The Human Soul Has Still Greater Need Of The Ideal Than Of The Real. It Is By The Real That We Exist; It Is By The Ideal That We Live" - Victor Hugo

"What Of Soul Was Left, I Wonder, When The Kissing Had To Stop" - Robert Browning

"Every Flower Is A Soul Blossoming In Nature" - Gerard De Nerval

"Language Is The Blood Of The Soul Into Which Thoughts Run And Out Of Which They Grow" - Oliver Wendell Holmes, Sr.

"Karma, Memory, And Desire Are Just The Software Of The Soul. It's Conditioning That The Soul Undergoes In Order To Create Experience. And It's A Cycle. In Most People, The Cycle Is A Conditioned Response. They Do The Same Things Over And Over Again"
- Deepak Chopra

"We All Have Hearts To Love, Brains To Think And Souls To Be. Live Your Life In Your Own Way And Don't Let Others Judge You. You Are The Only Judge Of Your Life" - Nishan Panwar

"Music Washes Away From The Soul The Dust Of Everyday Life" - Bethold Auerbach

"Nowhere Can Man Find A Quieter Or More Untroubled Retreat Than In His Own Soul"
- Marcus Aurelius

"My Mouth Is Full Of Decayed Teeth And My Soul Of Decayed Ambitions" - James Joyce

"Yes, It Was Love At First Sight. I Feel That After All These Years, I Have Finally Found My Soul Mate" - Barbara Hershey

"The Aim Of Literary Ambition Is To Demonstrate One's Greatness Of Soul"
- Mason Cooley

"Your Eyes Show The Strength Of Your Soul"
- Paulo Coelho

"In A Real Dark Night Of The Soul, It Is Always Three O'clock In The Morning, Day After Day"
- F. Scott Fitzgerald

"Women, If The Soul Of The Nation Is To Be Saved, I Believe That You Must Become Its Soul" - Coretta Scott King

"You See, You Are A Spirit, You Have A Soul, And You Live In A Body. You Have Emotions, You Have Thoughts, You Have A Will, And You Have A Conscience. You Are A Complex Being! And Jesus Came To Heal Every Single Part Of You. There's Not One Part That He Doesn't Want To Make Completely Whole"
- Joyce Meyer

"I Have Seen The King With A Face Of Glory, He Who Is The Eye And The Sun Of Heaven, He Who Is The Companion And Healer Of All Beings, He Who Is The Soul And The Universe That Births Souls" - Rumi

"You Can Take No Credit For Beauty At Sixteen. But If You Are Beautiful At Sixty, It Will Be Your Soul's Own Doing" - Marie Stopes

"Such Is The Foolishness Of Man To Offer
Another Material Wealth To Locate The Secret
Hiding Place Of One's Own Soul, Especially
When The Only True Guardian Who Can
Unlock Its Residence, Is One's Self"
- Richard Marvin Voigt

"My Entire Soul Is A Cry, And All My Work Is A
Commentary On That Cry"
- Nikos Kazantzakis

"The Road To Your Soul Is Through
Your Heart" - Gary Zukav

"Ordinary Riches Can Be Stolen' Real Riches
Cannot. In Your Soul Are Infinitely Precious
Things That Cannot Be Taken From You"
- Oscar Wilde

"Every Artist Dips His Brush In His Own Soul,
And Paints His Own Nature Into His Pictures"
- Henry Ward Beecher

"It Is Never Too Late To Put Your Heart And
Soul Into Anything Positive That You Cherish,
Relationships, Friendships, Etc. All Is For The
Giving And All Is For The Taking"
- Gebru Villars

"Love Makes You Soul Crawl Out From Its Hiding Place" - Zora Neale Hurston

"Let Us Not Listen To Those Who Think We Ought To Be Angry With Our Enemies, And Who Believe This To Be Great And Manly. Nothing Is So Praiseworthy, Nothing So Clearly Shows A Great And Noble Soul, As Clemency And Readiness To Forgive"
- Marcus Tullius Cicero

"There Is Only One Home To The Life Of A River-Mussel; There Is Only One Home To The Life Of A Tortoise; There Is Only One Shell To The Soul Of Man: There Is Only One World To The Spirit Of Our Race. If That World Leaves Its Course And Smashes On Boulders Of The Great Void, Whose World Will Give Us Shelter"
- Wole Soyinka

"I See Myself As An Intelligent, Sensitive Human, With The Soul Of A Clown Which Forces Me To Blow It At The Most Important Moments" - Jim Morrison

"It Is Better To Cry Than To Be Angry, Because Anger Hurts Other, While Tears Flow Silently Through The Soul And Cleanses The Heart"
- Pope John Paul

"Love Is Composed Of A Single Soul Inhabiting Two Bodies" - Aristotle

"The Human Voice Is The Organ Of The Soul" - Henry Wadsworth Longfellow

"Hope Is The Thing With Feathers That Perches In The Soul - And Sings The Tunes Without The Words - And Never Stops At All" - Emily Dickinson

"Communism Is The Death Of The Soul. It Is The Organization Of Total Conformity In Short, Of Tyranny - And It Is Committed To Making Tyranny Universal" - Adlai E. Stevenson

"Gracefulness Has Been Defined To Be The Outward Expression Of The Inward Harmony Of The Soul" - William Hazlitt

"Forgiveness Is The Most Important Single Process That Brings Peace To Our Soul And Harmony To Our Life" - Nishan Panwar

"Poetry Should Be Great And Unobtrusive, A Thing Which Enters Into One's Soul, And Does Not Startle It Or Amaze It With Itself, But With Its Subject" - John Keats

"Diseases Of The Soul Are More Dangerous
And More Numerous Than Those
Of The Body" - Cicero

"What Light Is To The Eyes - What Air If To The
Lungs - What Love Is To The Heart - Liberty Is
To The Soul Of Man" - Robert Green Ingersoll

"Beauties In Vain Their Pretty Eyes May Roll;
Charms Strike The Sight, But Merit Wins
The Soul" - Alexander Pope

"I Feel In The Depths Of My Soul That It Is The
Highest, Most Sacred, And Most Irreversible
Part Of My Obligation To Preserve The Union
Of These States, Although It May Cost Me
My Life" - Andrew Jackson

"I Shall Allow No Man To Belittle My Soul By
Making Me Hate Him" - Booker T. Washington

"No One Can Fill The Void Of Happiness For
You, Only You Withhold That Power. And
Once You Unleash The Power Of Extraordinary
Bliss Your Soul Will Be Content With Life"
- Ritu Ghatourey

"Confession Is Always Weakness. The Grave
Soul Keeps Its Own Secrets, And Takes Its
Own Punishment In Silence" - Dorothy Dix

"Do Not Make Best Friends With A Melancholy Sad Soul. They Always Are Heavily Loaded, And You Must Bear Half" - Francois Fenelon

"A Human Being Has So Many Skins Inside, Covering The Depths Of The Heart. We Know So Many Things, But We Don't Know Ourselves! Why,, Thirty Or Forty Skins Or Hides, As Thick And Hard As An Ox's Or Bear's, Cover The Soul. Go Into Your Own Ground And Learn To Know Yourself There" - Meister Eckhart

"The Torture Of A Bad Conscience Is The Hell Of A Living Soul" - John Calvin

"Reason Is Our Soul's Left Hand, Faith Her Right" - John Donne

"Disappointment Is A Sort Of Bankruptcy - The Bankruptcy Of A Soul That Expends Too Much In Hope And Expectation" - Eric Hoffer

"The Soul Should Always Stand Ajar, Ready To Welcome The Ecstatic Experience" - Emily Dickinson

"Begin To See Yourself As A Soul With A Body Rather Than A Body With A Soul" - Wayne Dyer

"The Soul May Sleep And The Body Still Be Happy, But Only In Youth"
- Mignon Mclaughlin

"The Happiness Of One's Own Heart Alone Cannot Satisfy The Soul; One Must Try To Include, As Necessary To One's Own Happiness, The Happiness Of Others"
- Paramahansa Yogananda

"Music Is A Moral Law. It Gives Soul To The Universe, Wings To The Mind, Flight To The Imagination, And Charm And Gaiety To Life And To Everything" - Plato

"When Our Souls Are Not Hungry For Power, Fame, Comfort And Wealth, We Find Meaning And Purpose And Love Take Center Stage"
- Ash Sweeney

"Pity May Represent Little More Than The Impersonal Concern Which Prompts The Mailing Of A Check, But True Sympathy Is The Personal Concern Which Demands The Giving Of One's Soul" - Martin Luther King Jr.

"Wake Up Your Soul! Wake Up Your Spirit! Life Isn't A Journey, And It Is Time To Get Your Hands Dirty By Doing Something That Is Worthwhile" - Senora Ray

"I Believe That The Soul Consists Of Its Sufferings. For The Soul That Cures Its Own Sufferings Dies" - Antonio Porchia

"Blues And Soul And Jazz Music Has So Much Pain, So Much Beauty Of Raw Emotion And Passion" - Christina Aguilera

"Your Soul Is Everything Associated With One's Spiritual Entity Guiding Every Aspect Of One's Physical And Intellectual Self As Experienced Expressions That Defines Living Life"
- Richard Marvin Voigt

"A Blessed Thing It Is For Any Mann Or Woman To Have A Friend, One Human Soul Whom We Can Trust Utterly, Who Knows The Best And Worst Of Us, And Who Loves Us In Spite Of All Our Faults" - Charles Kingsley

"Any Man Who Does Not Accept The Conditions Of Life Sells His Soul"
- Charles Baudelaire

"All The Riches Of The World Are Not Of Sufficient Value To Redeem One Perishing Soul" - Ellen G. White

"Invest In The Human Soul. Who Knows, It Might Be A Diamond In The Rough"
- Mary Mcleod Bethune

"Money Is Not Required To Buy One Necessity Of The Soul" - Henry David Thoreau

"Suppose You Could Gain Everything In The Whole World, And Lost Your Soul. Was It Worth It?" - Billy Graham

"Fear Is, I Believe, A Most Effective Tool In Destroying The Soul Of An Individual - And The Soul Of A People" - Anwar Sadat

"I Am No Longer Sure Of Anything. If I Satiate My Desires, I Sin But I Deliver Myself From Them; If I Refuse To Satisfy Them, They Infect The Whole Soul" - Jean-Paul Sartre

"With Every Breath, Your Soul Constantly Taps The Infinite Core Of Energy Equity That Universally Resides In Your Personal Life Expansion That Also Touches The Hearts And Minds Of Others" - Richard Marvin Voigt

"O My God, What Must A Soul Be Like When It Is In This State! It Longs To Be All One Tongue With Which To Praise The Lord. It Utters A Thousand Pious Follies, In A Continuous Endeavor To Please Him Who Thus Possesses It" - Saint Teresa Of Avila

"My Purpose... To Go On With My Heart And
Soul, Devoting All My Energies To Girl Scouts,
And Heart And Hand With Them, We Will Make
Our Lives And The Lives Of The Future Girls
Happy, Healthy And Holy"
- Juliette Gordon Low

"The Soul, Like The Body, Lives By What
It Feeds On" - Josiah Gilbert Holland

"Beauty Awakens The Soul To Act"
- Dante Alighieri

"A Soul Which Gives Itself To Prayer,
Either Much Or Little, Should On No Account
Be Kept Within Narrow Bounds"
- Saint Teresa Of Avila

"When Your Soul Is Resting, Your Emotions Are
Okay, Your Mind Is Okay, And Your Will
Is At Peace With God, Not Resisting What
He's Doing" - Joyce Meyer

"With All Your Science - Can You Tell How It Is,
And Whence It Is, That Light Comes Into
The Soul" - Henry David Thoreau

"Your Soul Will Always Guide Your Thoughts
And Feelings And Reveal Its Intended Mission
Every Time You're Listening With Love"
- Richard Marvin Voigt

"Run Your Fingers Through My Soul. For Once,
Just Once, Feel Exactly What I Feel,
Believe What I Believe, Perceive As I Perceive,
Experience, Examine, And For One,
Just Once, Understand"
- Lyrics From The Band Reef

"May Your Life's Journey Lead You To The Path
You Seek That Illuminates And Enlightens Your
Soul In Finding The Meaning To Your Life"
- Richard Marvin Voigt

QUOTATIONS ABOUT
SOUL

Concluding Thoughts:

Ever success is built upon a preparing a strong foundation, having a clear vision, and taking positive action each and every day. If you've been searching for a new lifestyle, then you'll find this book directive and inspirational. You can open it to any page and let that page help you rethink possibilities, consider new ideas, open new opportunities, and ultimately experience a more successful and fulfilling lifestyle.

Every problem has a solution! Regardless of your current situation or circumstance, know that you have the power and responsibility to redirect your life in any direction you choose. Simply start thinking about and research the kind of lifestyle that truly appeals to your heart. Begin your new journey by learning everything you can about your chosen subject. When you make that commitment, you'll open more unexpected doors to unique opportunities than imagined.

"Creative Thought Is The Only Reality
Everything Else Is Merely The By-Product Of That Thought."
- Walter Russell

So why not start thinking **BIGGER? It won't cost you any more.** It all starts by never allowing your current life's situation, environment, or so-called friends to limit your path to a happier, healthier, and successful life. After all, whose life is this?

Make a decision to focus on learning something new each and every day. Begin attracting your ideal lifestyle by doing something you love and enjoy. As difficult as it may be, don't allow money to limit your dreams. Focus on the kind of thoughts that make you feel good. Once you learn how to control your focus, you'll have a great chance to see your dreams take shape. You've finally learn to harness the power you always had within, a Universal Energy stream that flows 365/24/7 in any direction your project your thoughts, Good or Bad. Want proof? The thoughts you currently believe and project reflect the life you're currently living. Therefore, if your life isn't happening, change your thoughts, and change your life. It's something only you can hold, visualize, and project, living your dream come true.

Find yourself a mentor and spend more time with people who truly appreciate, support, and foster your dreams. Life may be short, but the thoughts we hold can make our life wider and more fulfilling.

About The Authors:

Richard and Lynn develop creative strategies that paint dreams, sell ideas, & market messages   Together, they present a unique team-approach, working side-by-side, helping clients pursue their passions while sharing their skills and diverse expertise as authors, artists, inventors, entrepreneurs, & Internet marketing education specialists.

Teaching by example, they mentor proven self-publishing services, graphic design, video production, domain acquisition, and marketing research of behalf of their company, RIVO Inc., since 1997. They've created & produced hundreds of videos, self-published dozens of books on a wide variety of topics and created thousands of original works of fine art, while refining their Internet Marketing techniques, mentoring programs, and related business website development.

Their mission is to continually uncover new products and services, test new strategies, and network useful solutions with off and online entrepreneurs, small business owners, writers, local artists, models, teachers, students, and marketing professionals.

Their goal is to help clients create an action plan that discovers and connects the missing pieces of the success puzzle. The goals they foster create multiple streams of income for today's volatile economic climate. Their motto is: "Do the work once and allow the work to create additional streams of income for a lifetime."

Feel free to contact them if you have questions or would like to tap into their talents and expertise. They appreciate your feedback and look forward to hearing your success stories.

Contact:
Richard & Lynn Voigt - RIVO
I. M. Education Specialists

RIVO INC - RIVO Marketing
13720 West Keefe Avenue
Brookfield, Wisconsin 53005 – USA
Email: support@RIVOinc.com
Website: www.RIVObooks.com
Website: www.WisconsinGarden.com

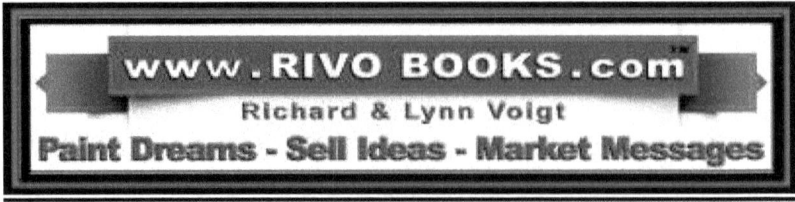

WI GARDEN – Let's Get Dirty
Our Wisconsin Garden Guide Promoting Delicious, Healthier Home-Grown
Fresh Food, With Tools, Tips, & Ideas That Inspire Gardeners!

MONETIZE YOUR SOCIAL LIFE
Earn Extra Income While Having Fun Online

FUNNY HEADLINES vol. 1
3,500 Outrageous Silly Brain Toots

FUNNY HEADLINES vol. 2
3,500 Outrageous Silly Brain Toots

JOBS
10,240 Career Paths That Can Change Your Life!

MONEY WORDS
Powerful Phrases That Million Dollar Copywriters Use To Make Piles Of
Cash On Demand!

GARDEN QUOTATIONS
400 Garden Quotes From The Earth To Your Soul

HEADLINE STARTERS
175,000 Words That Paint Dreams, Sell Ideas, And Market Your Message

CURIOUS WORDS
15,800 Words That Expand Your Mind And Change Your Life

INSPIRING THOUGHTS
That Inspire Happiness, Success & A Clearer Understanding Of Life

MARKETING EYEBALLS
100 Ideas That Can Add Unlimited Subscribers To Your Lists

SECOND OF FIVE
My Early Years- From Birth To High School

POWER PHRASES – Volumes 1-10
500 Power Phrases That Trigger Greater Profits

POWER PHRASES - PRO Edition v.1-10 (Complete Series)
5000 Power Phrases That Trigger Greater Profits

BABY NAMES – 2014 Edition
32,250 Baby Names with Origins & Meanings plus
Top 100 Names Of 2013 & 2,000 Most Popular Names

SEARCHING FOR SOUL
Simple Exercises That Can Help Clarify The Meaning Of Life

Thank you so very much for your interest and support in purchasing one of our latest publications. We always love hearing from our readers from around the world as to how this book may have touched you, your family, friends and business colleagues.

We would deeply appreciate if you would take the time to leave an honest and candid review of our book online at Amazon books. Simply, log into your Amazon account and enter the full title of this book.

Once the book title appears you will see a blue link that says, 'Customer Reviews,' Click it, and it immediately leads to a new page and a button where you simply click, 'Create Your Own Review.'

We recommend you create your written review in a word document first, making spell check and copy and paste quick and easy to insert, then all you have to do is click the submit button.

Both Richard and I would like to sincerely thank you in advance for taking time to leave your review on Amazon.

If you don't have an Amazon account, please feel free to personally email us with a copy of your review so that we can share it with others on our websites.

Simply email us your review: lynn@RIVObooks.com

We always look forward to hearing from you.
Lynn and Richard Voigt
www.RIVObooks.com

www.ingramcontent.com/pod-product-compliance
Lightning Source LLC
Chambersburg PA
CBHW071417040426
42445CB00012BA/1188